Holt French Level 1

Allez, viens! ®

TPR Storytelling Book

HOLT, RINEHART AND WINSTON
Harcourt Brace & Company

Austin • New York • Orlando • Atlanta • San Francisco • Boston • Dallas • Toronto • London

Contributing Writers

James C. May
Rufus King High School
Milwaukee, WI

Cover Photo/Illustration Credits
Background pattern: Copyright © 1992 by Dover Publications, Inc.
Mask/Ribbons: Scott Van Osdol; teens: Marty Granger/HRW Photo

All art created by Gary Otteson.

ALLEZ, VIENS! is a registered trademark licensed to Holt, Rinehart and Winston.

Printed in the United States of America

ISBN 0-03-054839-X

4 5 6 7   021   03 02 01 00

Contents

To the Teacher

Total Physical Response Storytelling (TPRS) is a communicative-based method that allows students to quickly acquire, internalize, and produce language. TPRS combines words and phrases with related gestures and a contextualized story to teach the vocabulary and structures in context. The ancillary package that accompanies *Allez, viens!* encourages an eclectic approach to language learning, and TPRS is one option that can add to the instructional variety present in every successful class.

The *Allez, viens! TPR Storytelling Book* provides vocabulary, suggested TPR gestures, and illustrated mini-stories that correspond to each **étape** of the textbook. These may be used at any time during study of the chapter to present the new vocabulary or to encourage oral practice of both the functions and the vocabulary. As students develop their skills in oral communication, you will find the results of TPRS to be highly motivating to you, as well as to your students.

STEPS IN IMPLEMENTING TPRS

The following steps are suggestions for implementing each TPRS lesson. As you become familiar with the process, you may wish to modify the steps somewhat to suit your individual teaching style or the different personality of each class.

1 Teach Vocabulary Using Gestures

The first step in TPRS is to teach new vocabulary by associating the words and phrases with physical actions or gestures.

- As you say each word, demonstrate the associated gesture. Presenting the vocabulary in groups of three words or phrases at a time will allow students to focus on the new terms and will facilitate retention. Have students practice the gestures as you say the words.

- After presenting a group of words, rearrange the order in which you say the three words to check comprehension.

- Then regroup the words by saying two of the first three words you have presented and adding a third word from a previous set.

- After students have practiced the gestures several times, have them close their eyes and perform the gesture for each word as they hear you say it. Practice the gestures and words extensively and assess comprehension by saying the words and having students demonstrate the gestures.

The vocabulary lists present the words and phrases in the order they appear in the story. You might want to group them differently. Some gestures presented in the Teacher Notes are based on American Sign Language. You may find American Sign Language useful for you and your students when creating new gestures for additional vocabulary.

Keep the pace lively so that students are challenged and focused on the activity at all times. Monitor one or more of your students who tend to acquire language slowly. Once those students associate the correct gesture with each word and have internalized the words, you may go on to the next step.

2 Practice Using Vocabulary in Novel Commands

Novel commands put the new vocabulary in a context that is slightly unfamiliar to the students. The commands should be as entertaining, funny, or silly as possible.

- It is helpful to have these commands prepared before class, perhaps on note cards. An example of a novel command with **manger** is **Mange... (la pomme, la tarte, le téléphone)**.

- After you have given students several novel commands, they can practice the vocabulary and gestures in pairs or small groups.

Since the *Allez, viens! TPR Storytelling Book* follows the content of the *Pupil's Edition,* you may not always be able to use the new vocabulary in commands. For those functional expressions that do not lend themselves to commands, you might substitute the targeted vocabulary and structures within sentences or questions.

3 Tell the Mini-histoire

After the vocabulary has been taught, students are ready for the short story (**mini-histoire**).

- Tell each **mini-histoire** using the new words and their accompanying gestures that students have now internalized. The stories give further meaning and context to the vocabulary and allow you to continuously check comprehension.

- You should retell the story several times, at first incorporating the gestures used in the vocabulary acquisition steps, but eventually relying less on gestures and more on the spoken words.

- Retell the story with slight variations. This will help keep students focused and interested. You can use previously taught vocabulary and phrases or easily understood cognates to vary the story.

Other variations in the process will promote concentration and enhance retention.

- Ask volunteers to act out individual sentences and have the class guess which part of the story they're acting out, or ask volunteers to act out the entire story as you tell it.

- Have students practice telling the story and doing the gestures in pairs.

It is vital to continually assess your students' comprehension.

- Ask true or false questions about the story.

- Retell the story with mistakes and ask students to correct you.

- Retell the story with pauses and ask students to fill in the blanks orally.

After students have internalized the new vocabulary and used the words in the **mini-histoire,** you might show them the target words and phrases so that they can progress from oral communication to reading and writing. The *Allez, viens! TPR Storytelling Book* allows you to make copies of the vocabulary lists, illustrations, and mini-stories, which you may give to your students as complete pages or cut apart to present one section at a time. You might give students copies of the illustrations or display them on the overhead as the story is told. You may choose to have students draw their own illustrations. Groups of students working together can draw stories to use when retelling the mini-story. Volunteers may then tell the part of the story that corresponds to one illustration, or, if they are prepared to do so, they can retell the entire story. You might cut the story into sentence strips and have students put them together in the correct sequence.

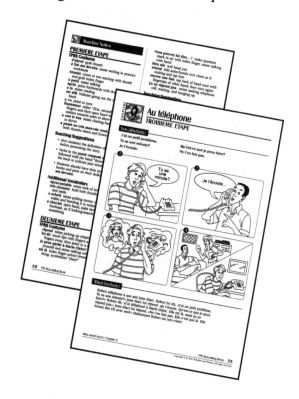

4 Assessment

TPRS assessment is constant and ongoing. If you choose to test using the storytelling method, there are several options to determine students' comprehension.

- You may list several words and have pairs of students use these words to create a story.

- You might provide the illustrations and ask students to tell or write a corresponding story. These might be all of a story's illustrations, all but the last in the series, or the first and the last only.

- Students can record their stories on audio- or videotape.

- Give students a vocabulary test in which they demonstrate their comprehension by relating French to images or to English, or by answering true-or-false questions about a new story.

- You might test at the end of each chapter by choosing approximately fifteen words from the three **étapes** and have partners create a new story using all of the words. At the end of a determined amount of time, ask each pair of students to tell their story to the class. You may grade each student individually on content, comprehensibility, fluency, accuracy, quality of sentences, and appropriate usage of vocabulary.

ADDITIONAL SUGGESTIONS FOR IMPLEMENTING TPRS

- For many vocabulary words, you may find props helpful. These might include stuffed animals, plastic foods, magazine pictures, small articles of clothing, toys, or anything you could use to associate with the target words and phrases. Although props are useful, they are not necessary. If props are unavailable, simple line drawings on the board can be used.

- It may be helpful for you to write target vocabulary words or phrases on note cards and color-code or mark each card according to **étape**. This will provide an easy reference for you later as students learn more words to use in their stories. You will know which words are new in each chapter and which words are recycled from previous stories.

- Students might find it beneficial to keep the words, associated gestures, and illustrations in a notebook. If a student is absent when a new list of words is presented, he or she can copy the words and gestures from another student, who might peer teach the story. You might ask that students who are absent write and illustrate their own stories and present them to the class.

- Students might tell a new story using the same vocabulary words, change the ending of the original story, add a certain number of details, or continue the story by telling what happens next. Different types of learners may be successful in illustrating or miming a new story, rewriting a story, writing and singing a song about a story, or creating a computer activity or a game with the story.

TPRS requires practice. As students become accustomed to working with the mini-stories, they will become more confident and more creative. They will build on their existing language skills and will have new and exciting ideas for TPRS activities. Capitalize on your students' creativity. As you get accustomed to TPRS, you will find many ways of integrating it into your techniques and methods of instruction.

Faisons connaissance!
PREMIERE ETAPE

Vocabulaire

Bonjour.
Je m'appelle…
J'ai 14 ans.

Moi, ça va très bien.
Elle s'appelle…
Elle a 15 ans.

J'adore…
Tchao.

Mini-histoire

Bonjour! Je m'appelle Thomas. J'ai 14 ans. Moi, ça va très bien. Et elle, elle
s'appelle Julie. Elle a 15 ans. J'adore Julie! Tchao!

Faisons connaissance!
DEUXIEME ETAPE

Vocabulaire

dit

J'aime…

le football

Je n'aime pas…

Je préfère…

le ski

les frites

J'aime mieux…

les escargots

J'aime bien…

le cinéma

la plage

Mini-histoire

Thomas dit à Julie, «J'aime le football.» Julie dit, «Je n'aime pas le football. Je préfère le ski.» Thomas dit, «J'adore les frites.» Julie dit, «Je n'aime pas les frites. J'aime mieux les escargots.» Thomas dit, «J'aime bien le cinéma.» Julie dit, «Je n'aime pas le cinéma. J'aime la plage. Au revoir!» Pauvre Thomas!

Faisons connaissance!
TROISIEME ETAPE

Vocabulaire

regarder la télé

aussi

écouter de la musique

danser

dormir

étudier

parler au téléphone

est triste

Mini-histoire

Thomas aime regarder la télé. Il aime aussi écouter de la musique. Il aime bien danser et il adore dormir. Il n'aime pas étudier. Il adore parler au téléphone avec Julie, mais Julie n'aime pas parler avec Thomas. Thomas est triste.

Teacher Notes

PREMIERE ETAPE

TPRS Gestures
Bonjour. wave hello

Je m'appelle... point to yourself and say your name

J'ai 14 ans. point to yourself, hold up fingers on hand twice, then the third time only hold up 4 fingers

Moi, ça va très bien. point to yourself, have a big smile on face

Elle s'appelle... point to a girl in class and say her name

Elle a 15 ans. point to a girl in class, hold up all fingers on hand three times

J'adore... pound fist on heart three times

Tchao. wave goodbye over shoulder

Teaching Suggestions
• Have students substitute their own age and name when retelling the story. You might also have them use the name of a celebrity instead of "Julie."

• Students might also continue the story by having Thomas ask Julie how she is feeling.

Additional Vocabulary
Il s'appelle... point to a boy in class and say his name

Au revoir. same gesture as **Tchao**

Comment ça va? mime shaking someone's hand

DEUXIEME ETAPE

TPRS Gestures
dit touch lips with fingers and pull fingers away to represent speech

J'aime... hand over heart

le football mime bouncing soccer ball on knee

Je n'aime pas... same gesture as **J'aime**, but shake head no

Je préfère... show two pictures of different foods (chocolate cake versus brussel sprouts, for example) and point to the one you prefer

le ski mime snowskiing

les frites mime eating French fries one at a time, holding "box" in other hand

J'aime mieux... same gesture as **je préfère**

les escargots draw shape of snails in air

J'aime bien... pound hand on heart two times

le cinéma point to name of a movie theater on board

la plage mime putting on sunblock

Teaching Suggestions
• Explain to students the meaning of **Pauvre Thomas!** before you present the story.

• Allow students to suggest alternate gestures where there is a chance for personalization. For example, some students may associate the beach more with playing volleyball than with putting on sunblock.

Additional Vocabulary
les vacances put clasped hands behind head and lean back

l'école write the name of a school on the board and point to it

le français point to French textbook

l'anglais point to English textbook

TROISIEME ETAPE

TPRS Gestures
regarder la télé pretend to "channel surf" with remote

aussi tap two index fingers against each other two times

écouter de la musique point to ears and then bob head as if listening to music

danser dance around

dormir close eyes and snore

étudier mime studying a book

parler au téléphone mime talking on the telephone

est triste make a sad face by pulling down corners of mouth

Teaching Suggestions
• Give students the definition of **avec** before you present the story.

• When students tell the story, allow them to change the story as they like as long as the context makes sense. **Danser** could be interchanged with **dormir,** and so on.

Additional Vocabulary
nager mime swimming

lire mime reading by looking at two open hands touching

voyager mime carrying a suitcase

faire le ménage mime dusting off desk

Vocabulaire

la biologie   l'algèbre   l'informatique

Moi, non.   Moi, pas trop.   les devoirs

la chimie   le sport

Mini-histoire

Salut! Je m'appelle François. Tu aimes la biologie? Moi, non, mais j'aime bien la chimie. Tu aimes l'algèbre? Moi, pas trop. Tu aimes le sport? Moi, j'adore le sport et l'informatique aussi. Et j'aime les devoirs—avec les hamburgers et les frites!

Vive l'école!
DEUXIEME ETAPE

Vocabulaire

aujourd'hui
samedi
le matin
a deux cours

à neuf heures
à dix heures quinze
l'après-midi

contente
demain
dimanche

Mini-histoire

Aujourd'hui, c'est samedi. Le matin, Suzanne a deux cours. Elle a maths à neuf heures. Elle a chimie à dix heures quinze. L'après-midi, Suzanne regarde la télévision. Elle est contente. Demain, c'est dimanche. Suzanne adore le dimanche!

Vocabulaire

C'est difficile.

C'est intéressant.

C'est super!

C'est cool.

C'est génial!

C'est passionnant!

Mini-histoire

Marie n'aime pas la biologie. C'est difficile. Elle aime bien les maths. C'est intéressant. L'histoire, c'est super! Le français, c'est cool. L'espagnol, c'est génial! Mais Marie adore l'anglais. C'est passionnant! Jérôme est dans la classe d'anglais!

PREMIÈRE ÉTAPE

TPRS Gestures

la biologie mime looking through a microscope

Moi, non. point to yourself, shake head no

la chimie mime pouring liquid from a beaker into a test tube

l'algèbre point to an algebra problem written on the board

Moi, pas trop. point to yourself and move hand back and forth to mean "so-so"

le sport hold up a picture of a sports magazine or point to pictures of different sports

l'informatique mime using keyboard and mouse

les devoirs hold up a notebook

Teaching Suggestions

- Have students retell the story using their own class schedules.

- After students retell the story, have them write a response to François. Have students agree and disagree with his opinions of his classes.

Additional Vocabulary

la physique point to physics book or a physics problem written on the board

la géométrie point to a geometry problem written on the board or to geometry book

la musique sing "la-la-la" and mime playing piano

DEUXIÈME ÉTAPE

TPRS Gestures

aujourd'hui point to today's date written on the board or calendar

samedi point to Saturday on calendar

le matin stretch like you just woke up

a deux cours point to names of subjects on board and hold up two fingers

à neuf heures point to 9:00 on a clock drawn on board

à dix heures quinze point to 10:15 on a clock drawn on board

l'après-midi have arm and hand turned down, outstretched, and lower hand slowly to symbolize sun going down

contente raise corners of mouth and put thumb on chin

demain point to tomorrow's date written on the board or calendar

dimanche point to Sunday on calendar

Teaching Suggestions

- Explain to students that students in France usually go to school on Saturday morning.

- You might tell students that **le dimanche** means *Sundays* (in general).

- Have students retell the first part of the story using two students, so they can practice different forms of **avoir.**

Additional Vocabulary

maintenant point index finger down to symbolize "right now"

TROISIÈME ÉTAPE

TPRS Gestures

C'est difficile. scrape knuckles together to indicate the concept of something difficult

C'est intéressant. rub chin with thumb and index finger and say "hmmm"

C'est super! hold arms up in air

C'est cool! hold one thumb up

C'est génial! hold two thumbs up

C'est passionnant! extend both hands up, palms open, and move hands slightly back and forth

Teaching Suggestions

- You might give students the meaning of **dans** before you present the story.

- If you present the expression **C'est barbant** from the Additional Vocabulary below, explain to students that this is a gesture used by the French to express boredom.

- Have students retell the story using their own classes and opinions.

Additional Vocabulary

C'est facile. lightly touch fingertips on one hand with those of another

C'est zéro. make "zero" with fingers and thumb

C'est pas terrible. motion hand in a "so-so" gesture

C'est pas super. throw hand forward and shake head no

C'est barbant. rub side of face with back of hand where a beard would normally be

C'est nul. pretend to push something off desk to show it's worthless

Tout pour la rentrée
PREMIERE ETAPE

le sac à dos

une trousse

une calculatrice

des stylos

une gomme

un livre

un taille-crayon

un classeur

un crayon

Mini-histoire

Dans le sac à dos de Caroline, il y a une trousse, une calculatrice, des stylos, une gomme, six livres, un taille-crayon et deux classeurs. Karim a aussi un sac à dos. Dans le sac à dos de Karim, il y a un crayon et... du chocolat!

Tout pour la rentrée
DEUXIEME ETAPE

Vocabulaire

Il voudrait acheter…
ces baskets
noir(s)/noire(s)
blanc(s)/blanche(s)

ce jean
bleu(s)/bleue(s)
cette montre

vert(s)/verte(s)
ce disque compact
cet ordinateur

Mini-histoire

Serge est dans un magasin. Il voudrait acheter ces baskets noires et blanches.
Il voudrait acheter ce jean bleu et ce jean noir aussi. Serge adore faire les
magasins! Il voudrait aussi acheter cette montre verte, ce disque compact et
cet ordinateur, mais il a seulement 50 francs. Il est triste.

3 Tout pour la rentrée
TROISIEME ETAPE

Vocabulaire

Pardon.	90
C'est combien?	200
répond	Merci.

Mini-histoire

Marie-Claire est dans un magasin. Elle dit, «Pardon, monsieur. Ce portefeuille bleu, c'est combien?» M. Martin répond, «90 francs.» Marie-Claire dit, «Et ce portefeuille blanc, c'est combien?» M. Martin répond, «200 francs.» Marie-Claire dit, «Merci, monsieur, mais il me faut un portefeuille noir!» M. Martin n'est pas content.

Teacher Notes

PREMIERE ETAPE

TPRS Gestures

le sac à dos touch back and point to backpack

une trousse mime zipping up pencil case

une calculatrice mime holding calculator and pushing buttons

des stylos hold up or point to some pens

une gomme hold up or point to eraser

un livre put both hands together; then open them, keeping little fingers together as if opening a book

un taille-crayon mime sharpening pencil

un classeur mime pulling apart binder rings with index fingers

un crayon hold up or point to pencil

Teaching Suggestions

- Give students the definition of **dans** and **il y a** before you present the story.

- You might use actual classroom items to present the story.

Additional Vocabulary

des feuilles de papier hold up or point to pieces of paper

un cahier hold up or point to notebook

une règle hold up index fingers about a foot apart and make shape of a ruler

DEUXIEME ETAPE

TPRS Gestures

Il voudrait acheter... mime counting money out for a cashier, smiling

ces baskets point to athletic shoes

noir(s)/noire(s) point to or hold up black piece of paper

blanc(s)/blanche(s) point to or hold up white piece of paper

ce jean point to jeans

bleu(s)/bleue(s) point to or hold up blue piece of paper

cette montre touch watch or tap wrist with index finger to show where watch would be

vert(s)/verte(s) point to or hold up green piece of paper

ce disque compact approximate the size of a CD with hands and then mime listening to music

cet ordinateur point to computer in classroom or drawing on board

Teaching Suggestions

- Give students the definition of **seulement** before presenting the story. You might also remind them that **triste** means *sad.*

- Tell students beforehand how the value of the franc compares to the dollar, doing some quick conversion problems to make sure students understand. You might also use the euro as the currency.

- You might switch items and colors when retelling the story so students have more practice with adjective agreement.

- You might add **ce jean-là** to the story so students can see the contrast with adding **là.**

Additional Vocabulary

ce short use hands to mark place on leg where shorts would end and make chopping motion against leg

ce roman point to novel

ce portefeuille touch pocket or purse where one would normally carry a wallet or mime opening a wallet

TROISIEME ETAPE

TPRS Gestures

Pardon. mime getting someone's attention by tapping them on the shoulder

C'est combien? point to price tag with question mark on it

répond touch fingers to lips, pull fingers away, and bring fingers back to lips

90 show nine fingers, then make a "0" with fingers

200 make a letter "C" twice with fingers ("C" is the Roman numeral for one hundred.)

Merci. move tips of fingers away from mouth, almost like you're throwing someone a kiss to say "thank you"

Teaching Suggestion

- You should have a price tag drawn on the board or transparency with a question mark on it.

Additional Vocabulary

Excusez-moi. same gesture as **pardon**

60 show six fingers, then make a "0" with the fingers

80 show eight fingers, then make a "0" with the fingers

Sports et passe-temps
PREMIERE ETAPE

Vocabulaire

jouer au foot
pas tellement
faire du roller en ligne
pas beaucoup

faire des photos
pas du tout
faire du jogging
jouer à des jeux vidéo

faire un pique-nique
beaucoup
manger

Mini-histoire

Après l'école, est-ce que Nicolas aime jouer au foot? Pas tellement. Il aime
faire du roller en ligne? Pas beaucoup. Il aime faire des photos? Pas du tout.
Il aime faire du jogging? Non, pas beaucoup. Il aime jouer à des jeux vidéo?
Non, pas tellement. Il aime faire un pique-nique? Oui, beaucoup! Nicolas
adore manger!

Sports et passe-temps
DEUXIEME ETAPE

Vocabulaire

Qu'est-ce que tu fais comme sport?
au printemps
il pleut
en été

il fait chaud
en automne
il fait frais

en hiver
il fait froid
il neige

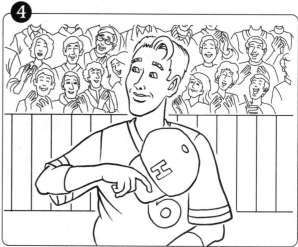

Mini-histoire

Qu'est-ce que tu fais comme sport? Marc adore jouer au base-ball. Il joue au base-ball au printemps, quand il pleut. Il joue au base-ball en été, quand il fait chaud. Il joue au base-ball en automne, quand il fait frais. Il joue au base-ball en hiver, quand il fait froid et quand il neige. Et pourquoi? Mais parce qu'il adore jouer au base-ball!

Sports et passe-temps
TROISIÈME ÉTAPE

Vocabulaire

demande

On fait du patin à glace?

Désolé(e), mais je ne peux pas.

On joue au basket?

jamais

On fait du vélo?

Ça ne me dit rien.

On fait de l'aérobic?

Bonne idée!

Mini-histoire

Serge parle à Suzanne. Elle demande, «On fait du patin à glace?» Serge répond, «Désolé, mais je ne peux pas.» Suzanne demande, «On joue au basket?» Serge répond, «Non, je ne joue jamais au basket.» Suzanne demande, «On fait du vélo?» Serge répond, «Ça ne me dit rien.» Suzanne dit, «On fait de l'aérobic?» Serge répond, «Bonne idée! Et on mange des frites, du chocolat et de la glace après?»

PREMIÈRE ÉTAPE

TPRS Gestures

jouer au foot mime kicking soccer ball with foot

pas tellement make "so-so" gesture with hand and shake head no

faire du roller en ligne mime doing in-line skating

pas beaucoup same gesture as **pas tellement**

faire des photos mime taking a picture of someone

pas du tout shake head no aggressively

faire du jogging mime jogging, pumping arms at side

jouer à des jeux vidéo mime playing video game using joystick

faire un pique-nique mime spreading blanket on floor and opening picnic basket

beaucoup gesture "a lot of" with hands

manger mime chewing

Teaching Suggestions

- Give students the definition of **après** before telling the story.

- Allow students to show you a gesture they associate with a certain activity or sport. For example, let them show you the gesture they associate with **jouer à des jeux vidéo** and then use that gesture.

- Students might prefer to stand while they make the gestures for this lesson.

Additional Vocabulary

faire du ski nautique mime holding a water-ski rope and lean back

jouer au volley(-**ball**) mime playing volleyball

jouer au base-ball mime holding baseball bat and swing

jouer au tennis mime hitting ball with tennis racket

DEUXIÈME ÉTAPE

TPRS Gestures

Qu'est-ce que tu fais comme sport? point to cluster of sports and a question mark written together on blackboard

au printemps mime taking a stroll and smelling flowers

il pleut mime holding umbrella

en été make a sun with both hands above head and squint to show it's bright

il fait chaud mime wiping sweat off forehead

en automne make an outline of leaf with hand, then make downward motion with hand to represent leaves falling

il fait frais rub arms lightly as if trying to warm up

en hiver pretend to shiver

il fait froid rub hands together as if cold

il neige move both hands downward while wiggling fingers to represent snow falling

Teaching Suggestion

- Give students the definition of **pourquoi, parce que,** and **quand** before telling the story.

Additional Vocabulary

il fait beau sweep hand through the air in the shape of an arc with fingers apart to represent a rainbow

TROISIÈME ÉTAPE

TPRS Gestures

demande make talking gesture with hand, then make question mark in air

On fait du patin à glace? mime ice skating

Désolé(e), mais je ne peux pas. make fist, "pound" against heart at least twice, and shake head no

On joue au basket? mime shooting (or dribbling) a basketball

jamais make "time out" sign and shake head no

On fait du vélo? mime holding onto bicycle handlebars and lean body forwards

Ça ne me dit rien. make a zero with hand, then move hand away while spreading fingers

On fait de l'aérobic? mime doing a jumping jack

Bonne idée! put index finger to temple of head, then pull finger up and out

Teaching Suggestion

- Before presenting the gestures for the questions above, make a question mark in the air.

Additional Vocabulary

D'accord. hold thumb up and wink

Allons-y! point to door with both index fingers, motioning to "come on"

On va au café?
PREMIERE ETAPE

Vocabulaire

J'ai faim.

On va au café?

prendre

un sandwich au jambon

Désolé(e).

J'ai des devoirs à faire.

J'ai des trucs à faire.

J'ai des tas de choses à faire.

chez Fatima

Mini-histoire

Jacques parle à Karim. Jacques dit, «J'ai faim. On va au café pour prendre
un sandwich au jambon?» Karim répond, «Désolé. J'ai des devoirs à faire.»
Jacques demande, «On fait du roller en ligne?» Karim répond, «Désolé. J'ai
des trucs à faire.» Jacques demande, «On joue au basket?» Karim répond,
«Désolé. J'ai des tas de choses à faire.» Jacques dit, «On va chez Fatima?»
Karim répond, «Bonne idée! Allons-y!» Karim est très content.

Vocabulaire

le serveur

Excusez-moi…

Monsieur!

La carte, s'il vous plaît!

Vous prenez?

Je voudrais…

Je vais prendre…

la boisson

Apportez-moi…

Donnez-moi…

Mini-histoire

Dominique est au café. Elle dit au serveur, «Excusez-moi, monsieur! La carte, s'il vous plaît!» Le serveur demande, «Vous prenez?» Dominique répond, «Je voudrais un hamburger. Et je vais prendre un steak-frites, s'il vous plaît. Et comme boisson, apportez-moi une limonade et un coca… Et donnez-moi un hot-dog, s'il vous plaît. Et je voudrais aussi de la glace.» Dominique a très faim!

On va au café?
TROISIEME ETAPE

Vocabulaire

C'est combien,... ?　　　　C'est pas terrible.
C'est (19) francs.　　　　C'est dégoûtant.
C'est pas bon.　　　　　　C'est excellent.

Mini-histoire

Emilie est au café. Elle demande, «C'est combien, un sandwich au jambon?»
Le serveur répond, «C'est 19 francs.» Elle dit, «Je n'aime pas le jambon. C'est
pas bon. C'est combien, une pizza?» Le serveur répond, «C'est 20 francs.»
Emilie dit, «Je n'aime pas le fromage. C'est pas terrible. C'est combien, un
hamburger?» Le serveur répond, «C'est 22 francs.» Elle dit, «Je n'aime pas
les hamburgers. C'est dégoûtant. C'est combien, un café?» Le serveur répond,
«C'est 8 francs.» Emilie dit, «J'aime bien le café. C'est excellent! Donnez-
moi un café, s'il vous plaît.» Emilie est contente, mais le serveur n'est
pas content!

PREMIERE ETAPE

TPRS Gestures

J'ai faim. rub stomach

On va au café? mime sipping a cup of coffee

prendre hold hands out, make grasping motion, and pull hands back

un sandwich au jambon mime putting meat on slice of bread and topping meat with another slice of bread

Désolé(e). hang head shamefully, shake head no

J'ai des devoirs à faire. hold up a notebook and mime writing in it

J'ai des trucs à faire. extend both index fingers and "roll" them around each other slowly.

J'ai des tas de choses à faire. same gesture as **J'ai des trucs à faire** but "roll" fingers around each other faster

chez Fatima make "roof" of house with two middle fingers touching and point to Fatima's name written on the board

Teaching Suggestion

- Allow students to give Karim's excuses in any order as long as they understand what they are saying.

Additional Vocabulary

J'ai soif. hold throat and open mouth

un hot-dog mime holding hot dog and taking a bite

une omelette mime cracking eggs and whipping them

un jus d'orange mime squeezing an orange and drinking

DEUXIEME ETAPE

TPRS Gestures

le serveur mime carrying a tray with one hand

Excusez-moi... raise index finger and shake it a little as if trying to get someone's attention

Monsieur! raise index finger and hold hand up high, as if calling for a waiter in a restaurant

La carte, s'il vous plaît! same gesture as **Monsieur!**, then take index finger and lower it in front of you, as if reading a menu

Vous prenez? point to three food items and question marks written closely together on the chalkboard

Je voudrais... point to one thing you would like from the group of foods listed on the board

Je vais prendre... run finger over menu, stop at a certain item, and point

la boisson mime drinking a beverage

Apportez-moi... move open hand towards body, as if gesturing to someone to bring you something

Donnez-moi... point index finger away from body, then towards body, as if gesturing to someone to give you something

Teaching Suggestion

- Encourage students to add more food items to Dominique's order once they know the basic story. You might also encourage students to come up with unique food combinations.

Additional Vocabulary

Qu'est-ce que vous avez comme sandwiches? make question mark in the air and point to **au fromage** and **au jambon** written on the board

Qu'est-ce qu'il y a comme boissons? make question mark in the air and point to **coca** and **jus de pomme** written on the board

Vous avez choisi? same gesture as **Vous prenez?**

TROISIEME ETAPE

TPRS Gestures

C'est combien,... ? point to price tag with question mark on it

C'est (19) francs. point to "19 F" (or other prices) written on the board

C'est pas bon. shake head no while you're frowning

C'est pas terrible. wrinkle your nose and shake head no

C'est dégoûtant. stick out tongue and have a disgusted look on your face

C'est excellent. hold two thumbs up

Teaching Suggestion

- The items and prices in the story are taken from the menu on page 140 of the *Pupil's Edition.* You might refer students to the menus on pages 142 and 143 if you have them invent their own stories.

Additional Vocabulary

C'est bon! rub stomach and smile

C'est délicieux! lick lips

Oui, tout de suite. snap fingers several times

6 Amusons-nous!
PREMIERE ETAPE

Vocabulaire

Qu'est-ce que Fatou va faire ce week-end?

voir un match de football

au stade

faire un pique-nique

faire les vitrines

au centre commercial

aller à une boum

faire une promenade

au parc

être fatigué(e)

Mini-histoire

Qu'est-ce que Fatou va faire ce week-end? Samedi matin, elle va voir un match de football au stade. Samedi après-midi, elle va faire un pique-nique et faire les vitrines au centre commercial. Et samedi soir, elle va aller à une boum. Dimanche, elle veut faire une promenade au parc, mais elle va être très fatiguée! Elle va dormir dimanche matin, dimanche après-midi et dimanche soir!

Amusons-nous!

DEUXIEME ETAPE

Vocabulaire

Allons…

Ça ne me dit rien.

Tu veux aller au café avec moi?

J'ai des trucs à faire.

Tu viens?

Désolé(e), je ne peux pas.

Je veux bien.

Mini-histoire

Cédric dit à Annie, «Allons au parc!» Elle répond, «Ça ne me dit rien.» Cédric demande à Alain, «Tu veux aller au café avec moi?» Alain répond, «J'ai des trucs à faire.» Cédric demande à Sophie, «Je voudrais aller au cinéma. Tu viens?» Sophie répond, «Désolée, je ne peux pas.» Cédric dit à sa maman, «Allons faire du vélo.» Et sa mère répond, «Oui, je veux bien!» La mère de Cédric est super!

Vocabulaire

Quand?

Ce week-end.

On se retrouve où?

devant

A quelle heure?

A sept heures et demie.

Bon.

rendez-vous

Mini-histoire

Robert dit à Karine, «Tu veux aller au cinéma avec moi?» Karine demande, «Quand?» Robert répond, «Ce week-end.» Elle demande, «On se retrouve où?» Robert dit, «Devant le café.» Karine dit «A quelle heure?» Il dit, «A sept heures et demie.» Karine dit, «D'accord!» Robert dit, «Bon, rendez-vous samedi soir, devant le café.» Karine répond, «Oh! Pas samedi soir! J'ai rendez-vous avec David!»

PREMIERE ETAPE

TPRS Gestures

Qu'est-ce que Fatou va faire ce week-end? make question mark in the air, then point to a weekend on a calendar

voir un match de football point to eye while miming kicking a soccer ball

au stade do "the wave" as they do in large games

faire un pique-nique mime spreading blanket on floor and opening picnic basket

faire les vitrines point to eye and say name of local department store

au centre commercial point to name of local mall on board

aller à une boum dance around, pretend to chat with friends

faire une promenade walk around

au parc mime sitting on a park bench, looking at sun

être fatigué(e) yawn and stretch arms

Teaching Suggestions

• Encourage students to change some of the weekend activities when they retell the story.

• Have students retell the story using Fatou and a friend. Remind students to make all the necessary changes. (**Dimanche, ils vont...**)

Additional Vocabulary

voir un film point to screen in room

manger quelque chose mime eating and sipping beverage

Rien de spécial. brush something away

Pas grand-chose. same gesture as **Rien de spécial.**

voir une pièce point to a book of a famous play displayed in chalkboard tray

DEUXIEME ETAPE

TPRS Gestures

Allons... gesture as if calling someone over

Ça ne me dit rien. make a zero, then move hand away while spreading fingers

Tu veux aller au café avec moi? make question mark in the air, point to a student, and mime sipping coffee

J'ai des trucs à faire. extend index fingers and roll them around each other slowly

Tu viens? bend arm at elbow with index finger extended, then bring hand up, pointing to self

Désolé(e), je ne peux pas. make fist, "pound" against heart twice, and shake head no

Je veux bien. shake head yes rapidly

Teaching Suggestions

• Give students the definition of **mère** before presenting the story.

• Before presenting this vocabulary, you might review the expressions for making suggestions and excuses presented in Chapters 4 and 5.

Additional Vocabulary

d'accord hold thumb up

Pourquoi pas? raise shoulders, extend hands with palms up, and raise eyebrows

Désolé(e), je suis occupé(e). shake head no and then pretend to write something using index finger

TROISIEME ETAPE

TPRS Gestures

Quand? make question mark in the air and point to different days on calendar

Ce week-end. point to Saturday and Sunday on calendar

On se retrouve où? extend one index finger and make circular motion in the air

devant hold hand (sideways and open palm) in front of you

A quelle heure? make question mark in the air and point to watch on wrist

A sept heures et demie. draw clock on board showing 7:30

Bon. hold one thumb up

rendez-vous start with index fingers apart, then gradually move them together to represent two people meeting

Teaching Suggestions

• Review telling time before presenting the story. Students might change the times when they retell the story.

• You might give students a copy of a calendar page, so they can point to the days easily while remaining at their own desks.

Additional Vocabulary

Quand ça? same gesture as **Quand?**

Tout de suite. snap fingers once

Entendu. point to ear and nod

La famille
PREMIERE ETAPE

Vocabulaire

Comment est la famille de… ?

le père
la mère
le frère
la sœur

l'oncle
la tante
le cousin
la cousine

le chien
le chat
le canari
le poisson

Mini-histoire

Comment est la famille de Patricia? Elle a un père et une mère. Elle a six frères et cinq sœurs, quatre oncles et cinq tantes. Elle a dix cousins et onze cousines. Et elle a cinq chiens, six chats, sept canaris et huit poissons. Comment est sa famille? Grande!

La famille
DEUXIEME ETAPE

Vocabulaire

Il est comment?
brun(e)
grand(e)

intelligent(e)
sympathique
un peu

timide
petit(e)
pénible

Mini-histoire

Etienne est le frère de Denise. Il est comment? Il est brun, grand, intelligent, sympathique et un peu timide. Denise est brune, petite et intelligente. Mais elle est aussi pénible; elle adore manger des frites, surtout les frites de son frère!

La famille
TROISIEME ETAPE

Vocabulaire

faire le ménage
ranger sa chambre
tondre le gazon

garder sa petite sœur
débarrasser la table
promener le chien

sortir la poubelle
laver la voiture

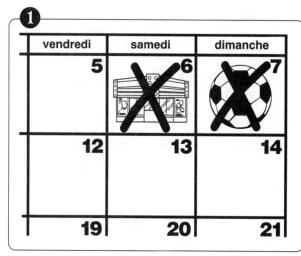

Mini-histoire

C'est le week-end, mais Philippe ne veut pas aller au cinéma. Il ne veut pas jouer au foot. Samedi, il veut faire le ménage. Il veut ranger sa chambre, tondre le gazon et garder sa petite sœur. Dimanche, il veut débarrasser la table, promener le chien, sortir la poubelle et laver la voiture. Philippe est intéressant, n'est-ce pas?

Teacher Notes

PREMIERE ETAPE

TPRS Gestures

Comment est la famille de... ? make question mark in air, point to family tree on board or to a picture of a family

le père touch forehead with thumb

la mère touch chin with thumb

le frère touch forehead with thumb, then lower thumb to about chest level to represent a younger male

la sœur touch chin with thumb, then lower thumb to about chest level to represent a younger female

l'oncle form the letter "O" with hand and place on forehead

la tante form the letter "T" with hands and place on chin

le cousin form the letter "C" with hand and place on forehead

la cousine form the letter "C" with hand and place on chin

le chien pat hand on leg as if calling a dog

le chat mime stroking "cat whiskers" on face

le canari extend the thumb and index finger in front of mouth and open and close fingers to represent a bird's beak

le poisson place open hand in front of body and zig-zag to imitate a fish swimming

Teaching Suggestions

- Tell students that in general, American Sign Language refers to a male with a sign above the nose and to a female with one below the nose.

- You may want to prepare a family tree for the class to point to or use the family tree on page 180 of the *Pupil's Edition.*

- Before presenting the story, you might review numbers with students. You might also give them the definition of **grande.**

Additional Vocabulary

le mari touch forehead with thumb, then point to ring finger

la femme touch chin with thumb, then point to ring finger

le fils touch forehead with thumb, then make a rocking motion with both arms (represents rocking a son to sleep)

la fille touch chin with thumb, then make a rocking motion with both arms (represents rocking a daughter to sleep)

DEUXIEME ETAPE

TPRS Gestures

Il est comment? point to **blond/gros/petit** and question marks written on chalkboard

brun(e) point to dark-haired male student and female student respectively

grand(e) hold hand far above head

intelligent(e) touch both temples of the head and mime studying

sympathique stroke hand

un peu show a "little bit" with fingers

timide put finger on lip and look down

petit(e) put open hand parallel to floor (hand should be close to floor to approximate "small")

pénible rub neck with hand to symbolize "a pain in the neck"

Teaching Suggestion

- Repeat the gestures for the adjectives several times with both male and female students so students can hear the difference in the forms.

Additional Vocabulary

blond(e) point to blond-haired male or female student

amusant(e) hold stomach and laugh

fort(e) flex muscle

TROISIEME ETAPE

TPRS Gestures

faire le ménage mime dusting off desk

ranger sa chambre mime making bed and putting things away

tondre le gazon mime pushing lawnmower

garder sa petite sœur mime patting young person on the head

débarrasser la table mime taking dishes off table

promener le chien mime walking dog on leash

sortir la poubelle hold nose and pretend to carry a trash bag

laver la voiture mime washing car

Teaching Suggestion

- Tell students what **n'est-ce pas** means before telling the story.

Additional Vocabulary

passer l'aspirateur mime vacuuming

faire la vaisselle mime washing dishes

Allez, viens! Level 1, Chapter 7

Au marché
PREMIERE ETAPE

Vocabulaire

un supermarché	une tomate	un poulet
a besoin de	du pain	une tarte
de (la) salade	du beurre	un gâteau
une banane		

Mini-histoire

Ousmane va au supermarché. Sa mère a besoin de salade, de bananes, de tomates, de pain, de beurre et de poulet. Il y a de la salade, mais Ousmane n'achète pas de salade. Il n'achète pas de bananes, de tomates, de beurre, de pain ni de poulet non plus! Qu'est-ce qu'il achète? Une tarte et un gâteau. Sa mère n'est pas contente!

Au marché
DEUXIEME ETAPE

Vocabulaire

Tu peux aller faire les courses?
Bon, d'accord.
J'y vais tout de suite.

une boîte de
un paquet de
une douzaine de

un morceau de
un kilo de
malade

Mini-histoire

Ousmane parle avec sa mère. Elle dit, «Tu peux aller faire les courses?»
Ousmane dit, «Bon, d'accord. J'y vais tout de suite.» Ousmane achète une
boîte de tomates, un paquet de sucre, une douzaine d'œufs, un morceau
de fromage et un kilo d'oignons. Mais Ousmane a très faim! Il mange les
tomates, le sucre, les œufs, le fromage et les oignons! Maintenant il n'a
pas très faim; il est très malade!

Au marché
TROISIEME ETAPE

Vocabulaire

dîne

Tu veux… ?

Je n'en veux plus.

Tu prends… ?

Non, merci.

Encore… ?

Je n'ai plus faim.

Oui, s'il te plaît.

J'en veux bien.

Mini-histoire

Laurent dîne avec sa mère. Elle dit, «Tu veux du chocolat?» Laurent répond, «Non, je n'en veux plus.» Sa mère demande, «Tu prends de la glace?» Il dit, «Non, merci.» Sa mère demande, «Encore du fromage?» Il répond, «Non, merci. Je n'ai plus faim.» Sa mère demande, «Tu veux des petits pois?» Il répond, «Oui, s'il te plaît, Maman. J'en veux bien.» Laurent adore les petits pois!

PREMIERE ETAPE

TPRS Gestures

un supermarché mime pushing a shopping cart

a besoin de hold both hands extended in front, clasp hands together and bring to heart

de (la) salade mime shredding lettuce and tossing a salad

une banane hold up index finger and mime "peeling" it

une tomate mime cutting tomatoes

du pain mime slicing bread and making a sandwich

du beurre mime cutting butter and buttering bread

un poulet flap arms with bent elbows

une tarte open palm of one hand and pretend there is a small pie in the palm of your hand, then take other hand and mime cutting the pie into wedges

un gâteau mime blowing out candles on a cake

Teaching Suggestions

• Tell students what **ne... ni...** means before presenting the story.

• Tell students what **non plus** means before presenting the story.

Additional Vocabulary

du lait mime milking a cow with two hands

des petits pois extend index finger to represent a pea pod, then mime pointing to the peas in the pod

des œufs mime cracking eggs

du maïs mime eating corn on the cob

DEUXIEME ETAPE

TPRS Gestures

Tu peux aller faire les courses? mime taking food items off supermarket shelf and putting them in a shopping cart

Bon, d'accord. nod, hold thumb up

J'y vais tout de suite. point towards door, then snap fingers

une boîte de mime opening can with can opener

un paquet de mime tearing off top of sack/carton

une douzaine de show all ten fingers and then two more

un morceau de approximate small quantity with thumb and index finger

un kilo de hold hand open and push up one time to represent "one" kilo or mime scales with hands

malade hold stomach and have sick look on face

Teaching Suggestion

• Encourage students to make food substitutions, like **une boîte de maïs** in place of **une boîte de tomates.**

Additional Vocabulary

une bouteille de mime drinking out of bottle

une tranche de mime slicing something with hand vertically in air

Je veux bien. nod head "yes" and hold both thumbs up

Rapporte-moi... open hand in front of yourself; then bring hand towards yourself to represent "bring back"

TROISIEME ETAPE

TPRS Gestures

dîne mime eating and then lower arm to represent the sun going down

Tu veux... ? use index finger to point to imaginary item, raise eyebrows to indicate a question

Je n'en veux plus. mime pushing food away

Tu prends... ? same gesture as **Tu veux... ?**

Non, merci. shake head no and hold hand up as if to "block" more food

Encore... ? offer someone more food

Je n'ai plus faim. pat stomach and shake head no

Oui, s'il te plaît. put hands together as if pleading for something

J'en veux bien. shake head yes while holding out plate

Teaching Suggestion

• You might change the food Laurent loves each time you tell the story.

Additional Vocabulary

le petit déjeuner mime eating and then raise hand to represent the sun rising

le déjeuner mime eating and then raise arm to shoulder to represent 12:00 noon

le goûter mime eating peanuts, a candy bar, or some sort of snack

Au téléphone
PREMIERE ETAPE

Vocabulaire

d'abord

a fait ses devoirs

ensuite

a parlé

après

a lu

est allé

a vu

finalement

a raté le bus

a passé un très mauvais week-end

Mini-histoire

D'abord, Robert a fait ses devoirs. Ensuite, il a parlé trois heures au téléphone à Marie-Claire. Après, il a lu une lettre de Marie-Claire... vingt fois! Après ça, il est allé au cinéma et il a vu Marie-Claire... avec un autre garçon! Finalement, il a raté le bus. Robert a passé un très mauvais week-end.

Au téléphone
DEUXIEME ETAPE

Vocabulaire

répond	est là	attend
lui dit	Vous pouvez lui dire… ?	encore une fois
Je peux parler à Marie-Claire?	bien sûr	Ça ne répond pas.

1

2

3

Bien sûr!

4

Mini-histoire

Robert téléphone à Marie-Claire. C'est la mère de Marie-Claire qui répond.
Robert lui dit, «Bonjour. Je peux parler à Marie-Claire?» Sa mère dit que
Marie-Claire est là, mais qu'elle étudie. Robert lui dit, «Vous pouvez lui dire
que j'ai téléphoné?» La mère dit, «Bien sûr!» Robert attend deux heures.
Il téléphone à Marie-Claire encore une fois mais ça ne répond pas. Robert
est triste.

Au téléphone
TROISIEME ETAPE

Vocabulaire

J'ai un petit problème.

Tu as une minute?

Je t'écoute.

Qu'est-ce que je peux faire?

Ne t'en fais pas.

Mini-histoire

Robert téléphone à son ami Jean-Marc. Robert lui dit, «J'ai un petit problème. Tu as une minute?» Jean-Marc lui répond, «Je t'écoute. Qu'est-ce que je peux faire?» Robert dit, «J'ai téléphoné à Marie-Claire. Elle est là, mais ça ne répond pas.» Jean-Marc lui répond, «Ne t'en fais pas. Elle n'est pas là. Elle écoute des CD avec moi!» Maintenant Robert est très triste!

Teacher Notes

PREMIERE ETAPE

TPRS Gestures

d'abord grab thumb

a fait ses devoirs mime writing in practice workbook

ensuite count to two starting with thumb and grab index finger

a parlé mime talking

après point backwards with thumb

a lu mime reading

est allé indicate going out the door with hand

a vu point to eyes

finalement mime "first, second, third" with fingers and then open hand in chopping motion towards palm to show last

a raté le bus mime chasing bus and waving to driver

a passé un très mauvais week-end hold both thumbs down and frown

Teaching Suggestions

- Give students the definition of **autre** before presenting the story.

- Verbs in the **passé composé** should be followed with the hand "thrown" over the back to indicate past tense.

- Students should have their practice workbooks and pens on their desks for **a fait ses devoirs**.

Additional Vocabulary

épouvantable mime look of horror

très chouette hold both thumbs up and smile

a acheté mime pulling money out of wallet and handing it to someone

a cherché open hand, palm down, to forehead, as if looking/searching for something

DEUXIEME ETAPE

TPRS Gestures

répond mime picking up telephone

lui dit touch lips with fingers and pull fingers away, then point to a student

Je peux parler à Marie-Claire? point to yourself and mime talking with hand

est là index finger points towards something; symbolizes "there"

Vous pouvez lui dire... ? make question mark in air with index finger, mime talking with hand

bien sûr nod head yes

attend fold arms/hands over chest as if waiting and tap foot

encore une fois tap back of hand once with fingertips of other hand; then once again

Ça ne répond pas. mime making telephone call, waiting, and hanging up

Teaching Suggestion

- When presenting expressions used on the telephone, mime punching buttons on the phone before making the gesture.

Additional Vocabulary

Je peux laisser un message? make question mark in air, mime taking notes on a small notepad

C'est occupé. mime dialing phone and then make busy signal sound

TROISIEME ETAPE

TPRS Gestures

J'ai un petit problème. show thumb and index finger almost together to show "a little bit" and scratch temple

Tu as une minute? hold up index finger

Je t'écoute. point to ear

Qu'est-ce que je peux faire? shrug shoulders while extending hands out, palms up

Ne t'en fais pas. throw open hand forward as if saying "Forget about it."

Teaching Suggestions

- Before presenting the story, have students recall what they learned about Robert and Marie-Claire from the previous two **étapes**.

- Have students imagine a different ending to this story. Marie-Claire is not with Jean-Marc, and Jean-Marc offers advice to his friend Robert. Have students use expressions from page 247 of the *Pupil's Edition* in their revised versions.

Additional Vocabulary

Qu'est-ce que tu me conseilles? point to student, make question mark in the air, and point back to self

Oublie-le/-la/-les! point to temples with fingers, then snap fingers

Ça va aller mieux! mime frowning, then curve mouth into a smile with fingers

Dans un magasin de vêtements
PREMIERE ETAPE

Vocabulaire

ne sait pas quoi mettre
porte
un cardigan
des bottes

un bracelet
mets
un pantalon

des sandales
un chemisier
une robe

Mini-histoire

Lise ne sait pas quoi mettre pour aller à la boum de Daniel. Maintenant,
elle porte un jean, un cardigan, des bottes et un bracelet. Elle demande à sa
mère et à son amie Caroline, «Qu'est-ce que je mets pour aller à la boum?»
Sa mère lui dit, «Pourquoi est-ce que tu ne mets pas ton pantalon blanc, tes
sandales et ton chemisier blanc?» Son amie Caroline dit, «Non, mets une robe
et des sandales.» Lise va à la boum de Daniel. Qu'est-ce qu'elle porte? Un
jean, un cardigan, des bottes et un bracelet!

Dans un magasin de vêtements
DEUXIEME ETAPE

Vocabulaire

cherche quelque chose
pour aller avec
nouveau(x)

bleu clair
choisit
en jean

à rayures
à carreaux

Mini-histoire

Jean cherche quelque chose pour aller avec son nouveau jean bleu clair. Il choisit une chemise en jean. Il achète aussi une chemise à rayures et une chemise à carreaux. Jean est très content. Maintenant, il pense, «Il me faut de nouveaux jeans pour aller avec mes chemises!»

Dans un magasin de vêtements
TROISIEME ETAPE

Vocabulaire

Comment tu trouves… ?   Il/Elle me va?   Il/Elle te plaît… ?
Je le/la/les trouve…   serré(e)   large
moche

Mini-histoire

Brigitte est dans un magasin avec son ami Pedro. Elle lui demande, «Comment tu trouves cette robe?» Il lui répond, «Je la trouve moche.» Elle demande, «Il me va, ce pantalon?» Il lui répond, «Je le trouve trop serré.» Finalement, Brigitte demande, «Il te plaît, ce jean?» Pedro répond, «Je le trouve trop large.» Brigitte n'aime pas faire les magasins avec Pedro!

PREMIERE ETAPE

TPRS Gestures

ne sait pas quoi mettre hold up several articles of clothing to self and pretend to decide what to wear

porte mime putting on several articles of clothing

un cardigan mime buttoning a sweater

des bottes mime putting on boots

un bracelet clasp wrist of one hand with the thumb and middle finger of the other hand

mets same gesture as **porte**

un pantalon put hands on both legs, run hands down from thighs to ankles

des sandales wiggle toes and mime buckling sandals

un chemisier mime putting on a blouse and buttoning buttons

une robe make chopping motion on legs where skirt would end

Teaching Suggestions

• Have students retell the story from a boy's point of view.

• After presenting the story, have students explain when to use **mettre** and when to use **porter.**

Additional Vocabulary

des boucles d'oreilles mime putting on earrings

une ceinture mime buckling belt

DEUXIEME ETAPE

TPRS Gestures

cherche quelque chose mime looking for something

pour aller avec show fingers "walking" together with both hands

nouveau(x) pretend to pull new item out of bag and admire it

bleu clair point to or hold up a piece of light blue construction paper

choisit extend fingers of one hand, palm up, and choose one finger by pulling it, then repeat with another finger

en jean point to jeans or denim shirt

à rayures draw stripes on board or in the air with finger

à carreaux draw checked pattern on board or in the air with finger

Teaching Suggestions

• Give students the definition of **pense** before telling the story.

• You might find it easier to teach patterned clothing if you can find examples to bring in and show to the class. Students could also draw the various patterns on paper.

Additional Vocabulary

bleu foncé point to or hold up a piece of dark blue construction paper

en coton touch or point to article of clothing made of cotton

à fleurs mime smelling a flower, plucking petals

à pois draw polka dots on board or in the air with finger

TROISIEME ETAPE

TPRS Gestures

Comment tu trouves... ? make question mark in air, pretend to hold up item of clothing, and raise eyebrows

Je le/la/les trouve... point to picture of masculine, feminine, or plural clothing items found in a fashion magazine, and give thumbs-up and thumbs-down signs

moche make a disgusted face

Il/Elle me va? make question mark in air, point to clothing item, and raise eyebrows

serré(e) grab arm or waist and squeeze

Il/Elle te plaît... ? make question mark in air, hold up clothing item, and raise eyebrows

large mime pulling up pants at waist because they are too "baggy"

Teaching Suggestions

• When presenting the story, you might use sock puppets to convey the dialogue.

• You might want to further practice **Il me va?** and **Elle me va?** by holding up several articles of clothing of different genders.

• Demonstrate the difference between **je le/la/les trouve...** by using feminine, masculine, and plural clothing items.

Additional Vocabulary

Tu aimes mieux... ? make question mark in air and point to either a pencil or a pen

Vive les vacances!
PREMIERE ETAPE

Vocabulaire

à la montagne   en forêt   faire du bateau

chez ses grands-parents   faire du camping   en France

au bord de la mer

Mini-histoire

Qu'est-ce que Laeticia va faire cet été? Elle ne va pas à la montagne chez ses grands-parents. Elle ne va pas au bord de la mer. Elle ne va pas en forêt. Elle ne va pas faire du camping et elle ne va pas faire du bateau. Elle va étudier le français en France. Elle adore le français!

Allez, viens! Level 1, Chapter 11   TPR Storytelling Book   **41**

Copyright © by Holt, Rinehart and Winston. All rights reserved.

Vive les vacances!

DEUXIEME ETAPE

Vocabulaire

part	un billet de train	un appareil-photo
il a pensé à tout	un cadeau	de l'argent
un passeport	un billet d'avion	il n'a rien oublié

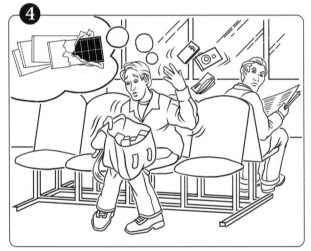

Mini-histoire

Christian part en vacances. Il a pensé à tout! Son passeport, son billet de train, un cadeau pour sa grand-mère, son billet d'avion, son appareil-photo et de l'argent sont dans son sac à dos. Christian est très content parce qu'il n'a rien oublié. A l'aéroport, il cherche son chocolat, mais il l'a oublié! Maintenant, il a faim!

Vive les vacances!
TROISIEME ETAPE

Vocabulaire

Tu t'es bien amusé(e)? Ça a été.

C'était chouette. C'était un véritable cauchemar.

C'était formidable.

Mini-histoire

Tu as passé un bon été? Tu t'es bien amusé(e)? Pour Claudine, c'était chouette parce qu'elle a fait du camping. Pour Didier, c'était formidable. Il est allé chez son oncle à la campagne. Pour Marie, ça a été. Elle a travaillé au fast-food. Pour Benoît, c'était un véritable cauchemar. Il est allé en vacances avec ses petits cousins!

PREMIERE ETAPE

TPRS Gestures

à la montagne trace mountain peaks with finger in the air

chez ses grands-parents make a roof of a house by putting middle fingertips of both hands together

au bord de la mer extend arms and look up at sun/ceiling (to represent lying on the beach at seashore) or make waves with hand

en forêt mime looking up a tall tree

faire du camping mime driving stakes into the ground to put up a tent

faire du bateau mime rowing a boat

en France point to map of France (either in the classroom or on page xxiii of the *Pupil's Edition*)

Teaching Suggestion

- You might change the ending of the story each time you tell it. (**Elle va étudier l'espagnol en Espagne. Elle adore l'espagnol!**) This encourages students to pay attention and also use more vocabulary.

Additional Vocabulary

à la campagne represent countryside in the air by using outstretched hand to show flatness of the countryside

faire de la randonnée mime hiking using a walking stick

faire de la plongée mime diving

faire de la voile blow on open palm of hand in front of face to represent wind blowing against sail

DEUXIEME ETAPE

TPRS Gestures

part use fingers to "walk away/leave" on desk

il a pensé à tout touch both temples of head with index fingers and wave hand over desk to represent everything

un passeport mime stamping a passport

un billet de train use thumb and index finger of one hand to "punch" the other hand

un cadeau mime handing a gift to someone

un billet d'avion mime tearing the top part off an airplane ticket and handing the other part to a passenger

un appareil-photo mime snapping photo

de l'argent rub thumb against other fingers of the same hand

il n'a rien oublié make "time out" sign with hands and shake head no

Teaching Suggestions

- Before you present the story, give students the definition of **l'aéroport**.

- To make the story more real to students, hold up actual items that Christian packed as you retell the story. Then have students use the objects when they retell the story.

- Explain to students that train tickets in France are punched (**composter**) to show that they have been used.

Additional Vocabulary

une valise mime packing and closing suitcase

Bon voyage! wave good-bye and blow kisses

Bonnes vacances! same gesture as **Bon voyage!**

TROISIEME ETAPE

TPRS Gestures

Tu t'es bien amusé(e)? make question mark in air, smile, and point to smiling face

C'était chouette. hold two thumbs up

C'était formidable. give a big smile and nod head yes

Ça a été. have neutral expression on face and use hand to make gesture for "so-so"

C'était un véritable cauchemar. grasp both sides of head quickly and look distressed

Teaching Suggestion

- Have students ask some classmates what they did on vacation, and then have them retell the story with their classmates' experiences.

Additional Vocabulary

Pas mauvais. shrug shoulders slightly

C'était ennuyeux. yawn loudly

En ville
PREMIERE ETAPE

Vocabulaire

la boulangerie
l'épicerie
la librairie

la poste
les timbres
chez le disquaire

la pharmacie
des médicaments
la pâtisserie/les pâtisseries

Mini-histoire

Jean va faire les courses. D'abord, il va à la boulangerie pour acheter du pain et à l'épicerie pour acheter des pommes. Ensuite, il va à la librairie pour acheter des livres et à la poste pour acheter des timbres. Après, il va chez le disquaire pour acheter des CD et à la pharmacie pour acheter des médicaments. Enfin, il est très content : il va à la pâtisserie pour acheter des pâtisseries!

En ville
DEUXIEME ETAPE

Vocabulaire

en bus   en train   **Il peut y aller…**

à vélo   en voiture   **en métro**

en avion   en taxi

Mini-histoire

Thomas va à l'école en bus et à l'épicerie à vélo. Il va au Canada en avion, il va à Nice en train et il va chez sa tante en voiture. Il va à la pharmacie en taxi. Et comment est-ce qu'il va à la bibliothèque? Il peut y aller à pied, mais il y va en métro parce que c'est plus rapide. Pourquoi est-ce qu'il veut y aller? Thérèse étudie à la bibliothèque!

En ville
TROISIEME ETAPE

Vocabulaire

prend la rue…
passe
devant

tourne
à gauche
au coin de la rue

près de
derrière
à côté de

Mini-histoire

Janine est à l'école. Elle part à 5:30. Elle prend la rue Lamartine et elle passe devant la maison de sa grand-mère, mais elle n'y va pas. Elle tourne à gauche au coin de la rue. Elle est près de la maison de son oncle, mais elle n'y va pas. Elle passe devant la maison de son amie Nathalie. Nathalie est derrière la maison, mais Janine n'y va pas. Maintenant elle est devant sa maison, mais elle n'y va pas. Elle va à l'épicerie à côté de sa maison parce qu'elle a très faim!

PREMIERE ETAPE

TPRS Gestures

la boulangerie mime slicing bread or breaking a baguette

l'épicerie mime holding basket and selecting produce

la librairie put hands together by little fingers to represent a book, then mime paying for something

la poste say **PTT** in French

les timbres mime licking a stamp and putting it on an envelope

chez le disquaire cover both ears with cupped hands to represent headphones

la pharmacie make a cross with index fingers

des médicaments mime taking medicine with a spoon

la pâtisserie/les pâtisseries mime eating a small pastry

Teaching Suggestions

- Tell students that **PTT (Postes, Télécommunications et Télédiffusion)** is an acronym for the French postal system.

- Explain to students that a green cross is the symbol for a French pharmacy.

Additional Vocabulary

rendre des livres mime returning books by taking them out of a bag and putting them on table

envoyer des lettres mime opening mailbox and putting in a letter

à la banque mime counting out bills

DEUXIEME ETAPE

TPRS Gestures

en bus mime driving bus

à vélo mime holding onto bicycle handlebars and pedaling feet

en avion pretend to fly with arms extended

en train mime pulling train whistle and saying "Choo Choo"

en voiture mime driving car

en taxi mime hailing a taxi

Il peut y aller... make fists with both hands and hold in front of you, then lower the fists while you nod and smile

en métro mime holding on to bar or strap to keep one's balance in a subway car

Teaching Suggestions

- Give students the meaning of **rapide** before presenting the story.

- You might have students retell the story using different forms of transportation to get to the various destinations. Encourage students to be as creative as possible in their versions.

Additional Vocabulary

en bateau mime rowing and adjusting sails

TROISIEME ETAPE

TPRS Gestures

prend la rue... trace the side of desk with index finger to represent walking down a street

passe place tip of index finger from one hand on desk and use other index finger to pass by it

devant put open hand in front of desk

tourne walk and turn

à gauche put open hand to the left of desk

au coin de la rue trace the corner of desk with index finger

près de place tips of index fingers close to one another, but not touching

derrière put open hand behind desk

à côté de point to the desk next to you

Teaching Suggestions

- Give students the definition of **maison** before telling the story.

- Before telling the story, make sure students understand what you consider to be the "front" and "back" of the desk, so you are all working from the same perspective.

- Have students refer to the map on page 328 of the *Pupil's Edition* if you have them invent another story using directions.

- Have students retell and act out the story with certain areas of the classroom designated as locations.

Additional Vocabulary

à droite put open hand to the right of desk

loin de place tips of index fingers far apart

jusqu'au prochain feu rouge put open hand out to indicate "stop"